BULL HEAD

The Selected Writings of Brian J. Mueller 1991-2001

Brian J. Mueller

D GITAL ALPHABET BOOKS

www.DigitalAlphabet.com

Bull heart: a personal and poetic journey through the process of divorce... /
Brian J. Mueller — Third edition.
Mueller, Brian J., 1973-
ISBN: 0996812032
ISBN: 9780996812030 (trade paperback)
ISBN: 978-0-9968120-4-7 (e-book)

1. Poetry

Third Edition: May 2016

Right there I felt it.
Now it is almost gone.
My mind let go of my body,
So my body wrote a song.

TABLE OF CONTENTS

INTRODUCTION

Several years ago at the first publication of this collection of my writings I wrote the following introduction:

> *The time has come for me to share a selection of the writings from the years immediately following my high school education. In the subsequent pages you will find some prose, and even more poetry. I would caution at times my writing is simplistic and may even lack the polish of more experienced writers. Yet I believe as you read further you will notice an evolution in style and clarity, which in the future I shall endeavor to develop.*
>
> *Despite the personal nature of these works, my intention has always been to publish them. As I look back over this volume of writings, I am sometimes a little embarrassed and surprised by my own naiveté. But if there were no merit to the ideas and beliefs I explore here I would not have undertaken such an effort to print them.*
>
> *As you embark upon these pages it is important for me to note that while my motivation to write is internal, my inspiration comes from my family, friends, mentors, and more. I sincerely expect you'll enjoy the material and any feedback you have is welcome.*

Since then my understanding of this body of work has changed dramatically. For starters, I no longer feel a sense of shyness or embarrassment about my work. As I prepared this text for publication in 2002, I initially wondered why anyone might want to read poems and prose about my experiences and feelings. I knew a great deal of the emotions I described are common to us all, but I did not understand the sense of community, of genuine human connection and understanding that can be gained through the exchange of words. Perhaps I was jaded by all the bluster coming at us from the airwaves and the Internet.

Today I am very proud of this volume. My goal was to make my writings available and accessible for friends and family. Little did I know that its publication would also symbolically mark the closing of one chapter of my life and the beginning of a new one. Since the arrival of Bull Head I have done very little writing, but I have not stopped feeling, experiencing, and challenging myself with very important questions.

It is true that everyone has a voice. This voice changes literally and metaphorically with the passage of time. Many express their voices through creativity and vocation. Others find their voice in more subtle ways, but universally we all need to be heard and understood. For it seems the silencing of this voice becomes frustration and quite possibly something worse. The writings in this volume are my voice for a particular period of my life. It gives me great pleasure to share them with you.

– Brian (2007)

PROSE

EDGE OF SANITY

I am sitting here on the edge of your sanity. Dare cross and your eternity will be altogether different. I do not promise me, nor do I expect you. Hope runs rampant in my world. Here you can be true to yourself, and open in your love. There are risks, and there are hazards. The price is no more than death, and the reward is no less than everlasting love. Step back and you risk little. I invite you to step up.

(*One more thing: Death is a peaceful love of blue-brown-eyed people with hysterical laughs and soft, gentle, meaningful features.)*

OUR FIRST CONVERSATION

If I had to describe her I'd say she is like the sun. She has a burning rough edge and stunning brilliance. Her passion is white hot. Her light is focused. Still, there are spots, little openings, visible vulnerabilities. These "wounds" pour forth her life. She is the Sun because she brings out the best in me, the Earth. I thrive on her light, and my thoughts spin about her. I long for her touch, but I fear the burn. However I smile because I know she longs to have her cares soothed in my cool waters.

She resists, I insist. If we could go it alone we would not need our hands. Idle fire spills from within her. Change comes so slowly, and yet time measures it fast. She feels spirits; she wants them to be free. She knows I am the one she longs to see…

BRIAN & HONOR

Tonight Fate smiles upon Honor and Brian. We, your family and friends, applaud the commitment you have made to each other and celebrate your willingness to follow a beckoning love. Yet let us always remember that love does not possess, nor would it be possessed. Love is a double-edged sword that demands you remain true to one another or suffer greatly.

Here's to you, Brian and Honor. May your love not become a rusty chain that binds you together, but a river flowing freely from sea to sea, soul to soul...

Cheers!

NEW ARISTOCRACY

We drank beer in the hot sun of a Reds game as the vendors hustled back and forth with their coolers and the umpires barked calls from the field which rolled out beneath us, our gaze falling symmetrically from the red seats to the yellow, green, and finally the blue where the wealthier patrons of the game sat idly chatting about their finances and sipping their margaritas with straws that looked like the peppermint sticks we would lick in front of a roaring Christmas fire. Among them was Fesum Ogbazion.

FURIOUS PASSION

She swims through the synapses of my mind, a very crowded place. I think about everything, and only her. She is not alone, but comes with much. And her absence – in that is much.

If I were to give her a name it would be "Passion," for I have none. I keep mine bottled up, never daring to let the light of day hit it. I do not need to; I live vicariously through all of her large nuances and extremes.

I love her, because if I do not I will hate everything. Hate makes me destroy; I do not wish to destroy anything.

Everything and everyone is inside of me. And I am inside of them. That is her secret; this is her saving grace.

SOUTHERN CALIFORNIA THOUGHTS

Everyone is trying to live up to this image. Only thing is no one is quite sure how the rest of the world perceives Californians, and so this image is somewhat unique and distorted among the people.

A GRAY HAIR

Like lightning across my brow, the gray struck. As I stood, young and strong against the wind, it sailed free. I did not notice it; a friend did. She quickly snatched my silver like a thief in a crowd. A moment of shock, a moment to blush, and a moment to laugh – gone. Now only the brown tresses remain echoing the fire within. Lightning will certainly strike again. Will I even let myself notice it?

SELF PORTRAIT (1)

He is really a rather simple man. Do not be fooled by the reserved exterior or deceptive smile. He lacks the ability to ignore his senses, though his rational powers are great. Never have I met anyone with a greater ability to translate the most complex of ideas or devices into simple terms for all to understand. He is a philosopher who can communicate clearly, a technician with feeling.

LEMON-LIME

They were out of lemons, and so she gave me limes. And it turns out that trying limes in my iced tea was one of the best improbabilities to come along in life. Having come to grips with this new taste, I am free to ponder the snaring of a woman's affections.

CORDIFORM LA BUTTON

I stepped off the sand and onto the strand. I looked down at my shadow and saw Caesar's commanding presence: the legacy of Rome alive and well standing fierce under the L.A. Sun.

That is what I remember most vividly. Except I can also remember the evening spent in San Juan Capistrano where the band rocked a small bar singing about lions and silver spaceships, not even whispering about the bag of groceries taken off the shelf too early. But I did not mind, at least at first. I was spending my time waiting, watching, and wondering. Time is not time when spent with good friends. We drank (me enjoying the best fountain cola I had ever tasted). I bellowed that I could not fight the feeling. My friends laughed, but they knew I was holding back. About that time a drunken miser stumbled on top of me, and it was all I could do to suppress the seething, yellow rage. Afterwards I sat in compliance, even during the conga.

My thoughts stripped away reality and I was in a world where women wore no clothes and I could breathe deep in self-fulfillment. And in that dream world lived the girl I had written on the plane (over the plains); strange, aloof, never fitting, like the wrong size screwdriver. And lest I sell her short, I must reveal that she, my first heart-stopper, possessed a beauty rivaled only by her intelligence. But I dribble...

Then I visited the only girl that dragged me to the edge of love. (Stopped cold I was, but I am still too young and inexperienced to know why.) Of course everything inside of me was present there, but I only noticed the sacrifices I made now and would in the future as I pondered my crossroads, especially that Western Path.

HEAVY METAL

Allow me to describe how much I miss California and the warm desire...

Heavy metal speaks volumes to the black masses. (You should see how brilliant the players really are! A combination of Gershwin, Beethoven, Copeland with Vulcan's fiery hammer, they rival the most serious musicologist.)

You can't fool me with that sharp-ass smile and rolling left eye. The smell is a tearing yellow, wet leather, and I don't remember your breath but I can see and hear you inhale, holding tight longer and longer until your lungs collapse and the sound in your throat grows louder and more excited. And I am reminded of your success in scaring me with that unanticipated response. For at that moment I realized why it is a man would build a castle for his bride, and why he would put it on the greenest rolling hills with ancient stones and the skillful mist everywhere clinging to the life that is her. Ah, but you paralyze my truest sense that lives on the edge of darkness and rages at the slightest injustice. Please don't stop me before I write a song for those demons of leather. Simple lyrics are all they need, and for you who want the straight and forward song without conjunctions, well, I will kiss you. No more plain and simple can I be. Hopefully when I bite your lip so gently, the smell of your breath like the musk in a damp autumn forest will extinguish this burning desire to flee westward and wayward. For in that heavy metal song of Harvard Yard love is the elixir that will keep Nebraska poets and saguaro prophets from ranging toward the setting sun and the California Seductress.

WAITING

Not even a simple "Fuck you!" But maybe you don't know yet. The waiting is killing me. All this bullshit about John Glenn, and I'm dying 'cause I might see you on the news. And the pain of not being at your side - you excited by the launch, the legacy, and the romance. Me, seduced by your mortality - a lust so primal. It is a gray day here. Nothing can fill my life like you, so I wander aimlessly through my apartment finding small projects. Finally I've had enough, and before I rue the day I was born, I set sail for the library. I crave the peopled solace and the solitude of my study. Why do I feel so anxious? I want to swallow it whole - the world, her, everything! Leonard Bernstein could not simply be a gay man. I cannot only be a writer, technician, teacher, handyman, lover... Take one away and I am gone. I am the gift life gives itself, the appreciation of so much diversity, the adroit realization of human frailty, and the conscious desire to become better. But oh the burden this places on my carbon shoulders. I want to be the man on television with the bourbon in one hand and the cigarette in the other, with the "fuck 'em all" cowboy mentality that sells millions of books, tickets, videos, whatever. And so this has become my everyday and my every night. I can't remember a time when I didn't try to devour the entire universe. Will I find salvation in her reply? Oh most divine creature please let me die.

I need a little hollow place inside my sanity where I can splash.

HE HAD ALWAYS BEEN THERE SHE THOUGHT.

He had always been there she thought. I know that I've seen him lurking in the distance. I can hear his voice calling out to friends. Why haven't I noticed him?

Suddenly she was standing next to him. Her heart skipped a beat. People must be magnetic.

He felt her presence immediately. He could smell her, taste her. It was a strange and primal feeling. The hair on his neck stood on end.

A simpler time, a quieter place, and the animal passions would have consumed them. Instead an uneasy awkwardness settled between them and an urgency developed. Speak now or forever hold your peace.

He swallowed hard. His dry tongue stuck to his teeth. Nevertheless he managed to utter, "Hey!" His hand gestured slowly, rising up from his waist. Eye contact had been made.

DAWN

The girl on the train said, "Why do you look at me so sexually? I don't demean you in the same way."

"And why not?" I replied. "Are we not sexual beings? Besides, you hardly know me, and I hardly know you. How many ways can you look at a person that you don't know?"

"I know you," she said.

"No, you don't. You think because you've spoken to my friend and travel partner about our trip that you know me. Is it conceit, or mere assumption?

"Before you get angry, ask yourself if I am really this pretentious, or if it's an act. Perhaps you feel you know me because you know my friend. You think I am either exactly like my friend, or the exact opposite. I would suggest the real me lies somewhere in between.

"So take a look. Is what you see sexually appealing? If so, get to know me better."

"What about you?" she said.

"Are you asking what I think of you, or are you interested in me?"

"Both."

"How about a drink? I'd like to get to know you."

"I'm not sure of your intentions," she smiled.

"Why they're the same as yours. You're looking for a passionate, intense, and deep love affair sustained for eternity."

She nodded, and I extended my hand.

WHAT TO ASK YOUR LADY

I suppose I would ask my lady what it feels like to be a woman, 'cause I would really want to know how she felt. If my tone was sincere, I don't think she'd offer me a lot of clichés. She might ask me what it is like to be a man, and I would tell her everything from the physical to the spiritual. I could tell her about the brute strength which courses through the entire body, by way of the veins in the throat and locking at the jaw. And then I would tell her about the helplessness a man feels in such a large and trying world. And I'd also mention that I have a hard time separating myself from my perception of things; even going so far as to forget my appearance. At times I have to remember what I look like to other people. I think back to the person I see in the mirror, and yet I still cannot remember if my hair is long or short, or even my eye color. I hope she would tell me things like that. In fact, I could tell her all about her smell and what color her eyes are, and the sounds she makes in my mind.

REALIZATION (1)

It is at moments such as these when I realize what is meant by "being afraid to live your life." My heart is so big, but the boundaries I place on it so narrow. Days like this one I feel as though I will burst. I must let myself be free, but the more I let go the more sensitive I become. My limits create order, but constrain life. Life is chaos, beautiful chaos. Stories have been written about humans full of love and beauty as well as anger and loathing. The force that prevails depends on so much. It seems that fate lies in me. Big days are ahead.

Life, grant me the ability to grow, the courage to lead, the strength to feel, and the faith to believe.

WHY DO GUYS LOVE LED ZEPPELIN?

"Why do guys love Led Zeppelin?" she asked.

Oh my, such an innocent and inspirational interrogative! Where to begin, my Muse? Please allow me to breathe these words in a simplicity befitting the subject matter.

Led Zeppelin is the sad song blues for men of Northern European ancestry. Genuine human sentiment combined with electrified rhythms borrowed from black mystics form the core of the Led Zeppelin sound. Men don't just listen to a Zeppelin tune – they become it.

Unlike the admiration and understanding of a Pollock masterpiece, Led Zeppelin is not an acquired taste. To appreciate Zeppelin is to revere the beauty of a woman and to feel truly alive. Take away taste, touch, sight, sound, and smell (all rolled into feeling) and the music is silenced.

Raw emotion and animal sensuality/sexuality burns in the lyrics. The echoing guitar and pounding drums drive the listener to frenzy.

How Many More Times*

Oh, Rosie, oh, girl!
Oh, Rosie, oh, girl!
Steal away now, steal away
Steal away baby, steal away
Little Robert Anthony wants to come and play.
Why don't you come to me baby?
Steal away, all right, all right...

Well they call me the hunter, that's my name
They call me the hunter, that's how I got my fame
Ain't no need to hide,
Ain't no need to run
'Cause I've got you in the sights of my..........gun!

Led Zeppelin sings to the average man, slave of this Earth, full of barroom passion.

Over the Hills and Far Away*

Many dreams come true and some have silver linings
I live for my dream and a pocketful of gold.

Led Zeppelin is a new day.

Stairway to Heaven*

If there's a bustle in your hedgerow, don't be alarmed now,
It's just a spring clean for the May queen.
Yes, there are two paths you can go by
But in the long run
There's still time to change the road you're on.

And then there is the poetry.

Kashmir*

Oh let the sun beat down upon my face, stars to fill my dream
I am a traveler of both time and space, to be where I have been
To sit with elders of the gentle race, this world has seldom seen
They talk of days for which they sit and wait and all will be revealed

Talk and song from tongues of lilting grace, whose sounds caress my ear
But not a word I heard could I relate, the story was quite clear
Oh, oh

Of course Led Zeppelin is wise to the wanton women.

Hey, Hey What Can I Do*

In the bars, with the men who play guitars
Singin', drinkin' and rememberin' the times
My little lover does a midnight shift
She's followed around all the time
I guess there's just one thing a-left for me to do
Gonna pack my bags and move on my way

Cause I got a worried mind
Sharin' what I thought was mine
Gonna leave her where the guitars play

And sometimes Led Zeppelin is bad as hell.

Black Dog*

Hey, hey, mama, said the way you move
Gonna make you sweat, gonna make you groove.
Oh, oh, child, way you shake that thing
Gonna make you burn, gonna make you sting.
Hey, hey, baby, when you walk that way
Watch your honey drip, can't keep away.

Led Zeppelin is the essence of a man and the sentimentality that haunts him. So take some time to appreciate their songs. Much of what constitutes a man is also inside a woman and vice versa.

*Source for *lyrics*: http://www.led-zeppelin.com

CRATERS OF THE MOON

How do I feel about her?

...Never has a woman been so adept or quick at getting to the essence of who I am. It is a vulnerable feeling, and so I am in love with her. She grips me and rips me with her dreams. The poet within me shatters like fallen glass. I want to hold her tight at Craters of the Moon.

YOU SHOULD NOT HAVE CALLED ME TO APOLOGIZE.

You should not have called to apologize. It only makes me feel worse. Your thoughts, ideas, and feelings are important to me. You bring me seeds and sow them on fertile ground. They become a wrinkle I cannot smooth for you. And that's tough, like falling out of love.

NO SUPERLATIVES

The Beginning

- No Superlatives
- Driftwood
- Klimt
- Running
- Wisconsin
- Swing Dancing
- Radio Head

The Middle

Transcend the logical
Logical but never give up the magical
Tough when you are sensitive to think logically
What is the "value" (under capitalism) in feeling?
[My gift of poems is not so "valuable" to you.]

The pleasure in meeting you is mine.

I thank you kindly for the note.

When I stop to think of Nashville,
only beauty comes to mind.

She told me she doesn't believe in superlatives.
She's the prettiest.
She told me she loves swing dancing.
She turned on Radio Head.
She told me she's from Boston.
She talks as though from Wisconsin.
She talks about running marathons.
She likes the idea of driftwood.

The End

Going places and meeting people is nice.
Running into you was serendipitous.
I am glad you are flattered.
I thank you kindly for the note, and I assure you the pleasure in meeting you and sending it is mine.
Nashville will no longer be a country music myth for me;
instead I'll be thinking of old friends, a newly married couple, and this girl who sounds like she is from Wisconsin, but claims to be from Boston (?)!
Now I must assure you that my intentions could not possibly have been purer.
I wish you all the best.

It will be difficult to find another person who:

- √ Doesn't believe in superlatives
- √ Listens to RADIOHEAD
- √ Enjoys Swing Dancing
- √ Runs for Fun
- √ Likes the idea of Driftwood
- √ Looks so darn pretty!

KEROUAC

Here I am driving through crowded streets. Shrubs, trash, cement, and buildings as far as the eyes can see. People are everywhere, too. Some seem to be going nowhere in particular and others can't stand the wait. And here I am with that hollow, empty, and lonely but in-the-middle-of-it-all feeling. And I'm wondering, no, I'm longing, to be the (~~last~~) only person on this planet. I'm dreamin' of inconceivable peace and calm. The only thing is I'm frightened to be alone, thinking alone. And as I turn left up the hill I pass a cemetery so green it's alive. I don't think it knows that it's supposed to die. And then I move on zipping by the dry cleaners and stop at the light by the DQ. It's tempting, but I put it off. I got things to do and people to see, but I forget all that when I notice a beautiful baby, just sittin' there by herself with no shoes. So now my heart starts to accelerate, and I am intrigued to no end. Everything's out the window except lost opportunities. I turn the corner, pull over; it's time for a dip cone. I cross the street feigning oblivion and the not noticing her not noticing me thing. I hop into line and end up with a Pepsi – guess I'm going to be thirsty. Like a failed mission I have fallen to Earth and step back into the crosswalk. But lo! Courage overtakes me. I turn and pop the lid off my drink and head towards the trash where she is sitting. He shoots, he scores! And now I exclaim in a general and raised voice, "How ya doin'?"

SHE MOVES SLOWLY ON DRY LAND.

I'm lying here and it is nearly 1 A.M. I'm almost fully awake 'cause I got two million things whiz-bangin' through my mind. I guess what has me most riled-up at this moment is the media followed closely by the human predatory nature which I believe is an experiment millions of years since gone bad. So with this defective DNA I settle into an evening of weightlifting and lusting for a girl who can't seem to find it in her genetic code to attack mine. Even worse is that my stuff is all over hers. And then some reason or logic circuit in my head 'clicks on' (cued by the trains outside my window). All this shorts my feelings, but I'm still a little miffed about the virginity thing, and that neither my friends nor anyone else seem to have any idea of the significance of love in a sexual encounter. Then when I finally clear my mind the late news show is all about violence as it pertains to rape. Now I'm petrified. Why are we such a sick species? [I fortify myself completely. Problem: with such definite boundaries, no one gets in.] Who do you like better, the locals or the popular leaders? I have turned this thing over and over, but still I am no wiser.

THREE NIGHTS

1

It's cold and I am running solo through the dark woods. My mind is moving towards clarity, my head is pointed downward. Such a strange thing is a shadow cast by the moon. It does not concern me long, for my thoughts turn quickly to my blue woman.

2

Two weeks only and I can hardly remember her. I won't undo the Marshall Tucker sounds and pretty girl smiles for just anyone. She is different, however. How can a brown-eyed girl make me so blue?

3

Xerxes Largo, a chocolate drink box, and a call from Dave do so much to calm this insipid dreaming. Drugs couldn't possibly work better. I know it. A needle never confessed its wonder to me. I stitched my bed spread with her rotten spells cast in casual glances, deep sighs, and overwhelmingly outrageous outbursts. But bitterness is not my drink - the lust is far too sweet.

Welcome to my new day. It is not really so new, but it feels much calmer and is like a forgotten rhythm - a peaceful one.

I am struck by the desire to write wonderful songs. How about something of growing up in Ohio? Or maybe I could put something together about a guy who smiled all the time. But my favorite would have to be about the young lovers and their quiet lust underneath the willow tree.

You got something you just can't hold.
That's love in your heart, but you still feel cold.
Like water in your hand when you squeeze, it's free.
Damn that girl – she ain't too sure about me.

She meets the world on her terms.
Everyday.
In the afternoon come rainy thoughts and impotence.
But I won't let them
touch her with a deep calm voice
All is put to right.
Watch out!
That cat ain't her - she's a stick of dynamite
I trade spices –
cinnamon, nutmeg, chocolate, just to be near her.
She buys them all for a smile,
in her heart a crocodile
Magnets she just don't understand.
She moves so slowly on dry land.

Feel the stream of consciousness.
Sex, money, politics, power steals the soul.
Sell yourself for some fame.
Wide-eyed children know your name.
Don't worry it will all fit on a zip drive.
Do I really believe someone will try and decipher this?
Sleepy.
Broad Road.
Need dry wall mud - least of problems.
Taxes.
Got to read a little before
I sleep.

SWASH

This is not a letter. How can I write when I have no chewing gum? For that matter, how can I write while listening to a song about a sweater. (It's not the sweater; it's the harmony, baby!)

I don't know anyone raised on a riverboat, nor anyone named Brunhilda. Of course this doesn't mean I never will. In this river town there is one helluva ripple. I've been here nearly every day of my life, and I still don't know exactly where to go to get what I want.

How would you spend your last Saturday somewhere? Working is a safe bet for the young and insane, but I must warn you not to undertake anything grandiose with one foot on the train. I know this doesn't bother J.Q.P., but if you are insane enough to work down to the last minute, then you must be looking for some closure.

Forget about good days, think of one that sucks. You felt good in the A.M. and then nothing tasted sweet after that first Coke. But it can all turn with the flip of a coin. It must be the fall karma blowing in on that sweet Zephyr. (I wish Zephyr rhymed with Sarsaparilla.)

Sometimes you can't escape Bill and his vicious source code (unless you're the type who wouldn't spend your last Saturday at work). But oh my sweet luck! This week I had a little brown-eyed, blushing Serendipity waiting for me. I can't spell it but it rhymes with tangerine.

I can close my eyes easily tonight. I won't be dreaming about this literary debacle, but of myself standing naked in the park, singing my favorite song, and hurling my favorite four letter words at the hecklers.

STONE MOUNTAIN

I rode the sky lift to the top of Stone Mountain. Admittedly the whole experience was not true to my expectations. The heights terrified me. Dangling helplessly from a cable in an aluminum box with thirty other people only intensified the panic. I grasped the rail firmly, and marveled at the four children next to me giggling as we ascended more than four thousand feet up the ominous mountain. (*Aren't little kids supposed to be timid, especially of new and grandiose things?*)

Atop the largest piece of exposed granite in the world I took a breath, and then started taking in all the activity. Americans and foreign visitors alike were engaged in various activities. Some explored the rock and others sat alone. While most milled about in the cool autumn breeze, the lovers sought small formations of wind-blown granite for privacy. Even if they were not alone they pretended to be.

While I strolled about the top, a thought occurred to me: who of this Earth would not wish to walk along the summit of a mountain on a beautiful day such as this? The vista seemed endless. Stone Mountain Park, an astonishing creation, is a wonderland of capitalism, in the same vein as Disneyland. Despite the contrived modernism of the park, after only an hour or so I am defeated and utterly enchanted.

As I write these words, a bee has come to rest on my yellow pad and crawling along the granite is an orange butterfly. To the west is downtown Atlanta. It is shrouded in hazy pollution. The clouds stretch endlessly beneath the perfect afternoon sun. And just maybe it is a little reassuring to have the stalwart figures of Stonewall, Lee, and Davis rolling out beneath me, keeping this rock from crumbling.

Below the giant relief of the Confederate heroes stretches a park and short path. Etched in the stones is information concerning the secession of states from the Union, their admission to the Confederacy, and their subsequent readmission to the Union. In less than an hour I've learned so much. But even more interesting to me are the many quotes from the grandest figures of American history. Never doubt the ability of humans to stir emotions and send a young man to battle with such words as honor, equality, virtue, morality, necessity, glory, integrity, principle, opportunity, promise, duty, liberty, prosperity, compassion, and obligation. In all these rocks not one occurrence of the word "love." I did, however, glimpse a "love" or two in the graffiti covering many of the stones located alongside the path down Stone Mountain.

Don't get me wrong, Stone Mountain is a great place. Here Americans rejoice, but other than listless lovers on the rocks, it does not evoke the spirit of life intrinsic in nature and the earth. At Stone Mountain you will only find your national pride and perhaps a great Fourth of July toast. I anticipated a little more solace as I searched for a place to ponder what I must do for the woman I hold dear to regard me as highly as she does Robert E. Lee. I guess I don't quite understand it, at least not one hundred percent. (*Somebody poured asphalt in the wind hollows of the rock!*)

DAYDREAM

She was my wife in another life. Or perhaps it was the other way around. Regardless, I can see us on green rolling plains the farmer and the horse lover. There are no children, but everything is bursting with life. Clouds roll across the skies with intermittent breaks of sunshine. The stones, the flowers, and the animals are all just a little damp as the Earth in this place is juicy and bursting with life's sustaining waters. The nights and mornings are cool but give way to warmer days. This is it: the beginning and the end. The world has only these dimensions: green, mist, and lovers.

Why must I castrate myself to achieve emotional impotence? I cannot pretend or be a part-time anything. Am I a modern warrior in the business trenches, or am I a passionate lover and writer of verse? It must be one or the other. I know what I'd rather be, but I won't let me. I'm afraid to fill that void. That VOID! (I tell myself that no one feels the same, nobody would be interested in the stuff I write.)

Fuck it all! I never would, never could. I don't believe it when someone claims indifference. If you have no feeling you are dead. But not dead as a rock is dead; a rock is the history of this earth and as such is alive.

No. A dead person, when still breathing, is a pathetic thing. How sad it is to those alive to see someone without hope, missing all the sensations like sand between the toes and cinnamon beneath the nose. How strange it is that we the living should be envious! You fucking lifeless bastards! You only exist to magnify our negative emotions. We don't even see you when we are passionately in love. (On a sunny day I forget about the Henry Millers of this world.)

So here I am at the brink of love with a woman I know completely and not at all. She has a home 17,000 miles away *as the crow flies*. (All these seductresses in my own nefarious land, and I am utterly mad for a foreigner.)

She is not the only one ever to get me, but so far she is closer to the eternal purchase than any other lady has ever been. All this said it is the same chipped tooth. My stomach hurts, my heart sinks, and overall I am lousy. God help those who must tolerate me!

Oh, how I need to dance! Demons in the walls come let me feel your techno beats in a trance-like oblivion! Show me the pale shadows of your faces as I cross the sea of anonymity, careful only to touch those with a slight pulse. I can smell the stench of the living dead and only the music can hold me. I want her. Eventually we are thrown to the street.

It is the same feeling for me. I want her so badly but the gods conspire against me. How can tomorrow follow this midnight of the soul? Nothing will save me. I will drown in a sea of tears, though not one shed. Instead they are suffocating me from the inside. Forgetting my feelings works, that's all. How? Why I get lost in work, that's how. I join the undead. There is no ritual. Just stop doing that which makes you live – *feel*.

The neo-classical human of impeccable virtue is particularly susceptible. Finding him is like finding a four-leaf clover. When found, the urge to pick him is overwhelming. Leave him in the earth!

I will not die but perforce! Take me from this Earth and put me on the pavement of a dark, dripping metropolis. I can tolerate the gargoyles and buzzards circling in anticipation. The stone weariness makes me harder but I can't fight the feeling. Thank goodness it is too late for me. In this brave new world I will have peace; I will have love; I will have solitude.

I can wait, wait happily without fear or worry. I want her. She knows that. Should the dead conspire to keep us apart, my goddess will surely appear in another shape and form. And this time we will have children.

WAR LOVE LETTER (DEAR HELEN)

I write to you in utter desperation and need. You must have an inkling of what I am about to say. Yet for as long as you have known, your silence mocks my heavy heart. I wait calmly and patiently, appearing the pillar of strength and virtue. (That is what you want, right? You need to feel safe and protected. You want someone who can shield you from the mixed sensations of life.) In reality I am a weir of emotion straining to control myself.

With your last letter came the orders that sent a thousand men to their death. Unspeakable horrors abound. For your beauty and the stewardship of your love a war is being fought.

You are not a victim in this conflagration, but your innocence is noted. How could you know your blushing smile would send the mighty Ares to his chariot? Who would have thought your kind heart with its soulful discourses and the morning mist of your kiss would be so potent?

I am helpless to stop the fighting. My job is to contain it and one day to draft an accord. Complete and total dominance by one side seems unlikely. Rather a stalemate will ensue and the spoils will be divided, you among them. Then all will realize your frailty. As always you will be cherished, but as disillusionment grows among the ranks, you will be forced to withdraw.

Step forward now. End this struggle. Tell me, tell me, tell me... I shall turn these arms into a monument of humankind. So long as the sun leaps into the morning sky, so long as the moon calls the tides, so long will I love and cherish you.

CONFESSION

Nail bitin' but the hands don't look too shabby. On the wrist is wet leather and what remains of the bamboo strap. He doesn't feel like doing this except when he's in love. Actually, he's never been in love – lust mostly. (The NASA pen is working furiously now!) And the one time he broke a girl's heart still causes that sinking feeling and a quiet rage. He was barely a man and not in love. She, a handsome and generally kind-hearted woman, was never idle in searching…a man always on her horizon. She worked in the forest setting traps. I don't think she meant to keep him, but sometimes you're not sure what you've caught. He was stunned, and in idle times a willing captive. Call her Dido, for there was no chance of togetherness. Let the similarities stop there. He so badly wanted to feel something. She longed for the longing of a man. No sooner than a beginning's end they parted. Her punishment was a scorned love. His punishment a shame turned inward and aimless searching.

TRUE DESIRES

It seems to me that we as people are fondest of that which we cannot have, or rather cannot come by so easily. Often the "pie in the sky" is prosperity, but capitalism has bastardized this elusive desire and now it has become greed. In fact there is little in this world we (Americans) cannot pursue in the utter certainty we shall succeed in obtaining it. Still, quite the opposite has come true as of late. We obsess in our wealth and are easily overcome by it. We have "too much of a good thing."

Good people are lost each day. It is not easy to decipher what you want and what you really need. I know. Many of us keep the answer in the darkest recesses of our mind. Alone with thought we are virtuous and free about our true desires. Like sparks, life triggers the emotions inherent in us. That accountant never wanted anything more than to be the leader of a marching band (*too silly, no money in that!*). That bus driver really, really wanted to be a law professor (*no self-assurance or family support!*). This politician wants to be a hairdresser (*freedom must be an illusion!*). And so it goes.

I make no bones about it. The truth for me lies close to the surface. Again, it seems, no one dares ask another for the truth in desires. I hold it close, but dig ever so slightly and you will see it all. I desire to be a writer, a poet, a philosopher, a man who makes others think, smile, and cry. And though I can scarcely imagine a sweeter life, all this I would gladly trade for the love of one woman. (I am American; must I sacrifice anything?) Work as a mole in an office my whole life,

I could, for that love of mine. Of course I would never see it beneath me to stoop to the earth to gather the food we eat. If she bids it, I will do it.

I plan to get off with a lighter sentence, and with equal depth of love. Nonetheless, that is my true desire: true love Tonight as I type this I look down at my body. It is sore as I am working hard to restore the strength and shape so recently lost. My body fights wars on many fronts, against many foes. I appreciate this. My mind must help. And so it shall.

AUGUSTINIAN DIALOGUE

"Were your other women prettier than I am?"

"You know there weren't many. Only one really."

"Well, her?"

"You must know?"

"I must."

"Yes."

"How so?"

"She was more beautiful in a reality whose existence I no longer recognize. You, fair lady, make me whole. Your looks are so becoming that the mere sight of you softens all rough edges."

"How can that be? You said she was prettier."

"True, but I wouldn't recognize her should I meet her in a crowd. For all I know her face is everywhere, and has graced the pages of thousands of magazines…or even daily flashes across millions of screens.

"Sure, she was prettier. Her eyes were bluer, her hair was blonder, and her skin was darker. But you, you my darling, for all your inconsistencies and 'unpretty' qualities, you are the more real to me. In your eyes I see every color. In your hair I find waves of soft silk. Your touch is the electric of splitting atoms.

"You are infinite, infinitely mine. Beauty is such a narrow concept that she was, or perhaps is, the more of it. The possibility within you, and the thrill of knowing not knowing, is my love for you."

…

"Give me a second."

"Why?"
"I think I might cry."
"Then why are you smiling?"
"Because I never know what you're going to say."

TWILIGHT

I think you're in the right, and still I understand the plight of the romantic. Ya' know there is this me that is rough around the edges. I've got this idea that I'm somewhere out on the plains. The sky stretches forever in a blue-gray-yellow twilight. The land is a fading dark green. I'm weary. The only thing holding me up is my old pair of jeans and my work boots. I stride confidently and rub my chin. (Which is rougher my hand or my face?) I walk into a roadside diner. There are a few people scattered about the place and the jukebox is playing "Moonwalker" by Santos and Johnny. I sit quietly at the counter. I hate coffee, but I order one 'cause I can't get rid of the salty taste in my mouth. Overcome with the haste of hunger, I hardly taste my dinner. For dessert I order a piece of pie and look dreamily past the old waitress. I'm tryin' to remember a time when she was beautiful and would've broken my heart. I stretch my arms quietly and leave far too much for a tip. I'm outta here, don't know if I'll be back.

I get into my old pickup and drive until I catch up to the horizon. Everywhere stand tall buildings in asphalt furrows. There is not a speck of dust on me now. I open the car door and step onto the black, damp street. A horn startles me and I look upward, searching for the sun. At the top of the stairs I turn around and see my car with lights flashing. I brace myself with a tug on my jacket and walk through the colossal columns and into the bank. The resemblance to a sarcophagus is uncanny. The shining marble floors echo with each step. Some guy with a gun and blue shirt eyeballs me. I curse his ignorance, amuse myself with the thought of giving him a hug, and join the line. My mind drifts to the mother of pearl clouds I saw in the desert and I want to buy them, or even just a puff of them, and give them to my lover. “Can I help you? Sir?” I’m standing across from a black woman. Her stare is absent. Her nameplate reads “Julia Brookes.” I’m not sure if the soiled check or my suit surprises her more. “Just a moment, sir.” She types furiously and then counts out $500. “Have a nice day,” she says. “You, too, Julia.” But I forget to wink.

DECEMBER 2000

The loneliness returned as quickly as it departed. It swept over me like the snow that blanketed Chicago two days ago. Only time would diminish this burden (and the determination to fill the void in my life).

Why does flying fill me with such inescapable sadness? The gentleman from Idaho sitting next to me on the way to Salt Lake City awakened romantic yearnings of the imagined West of yesteryear. You know what I'm talking about - the snow swept mountains and the flowered plains all unspoiled by man's presence and so far removed from the problems of our reality?

The girl in front of me pierced my heart with a blade of lust. Her flawless complexion, her softly defined profile, her lush flowing hair, and her abstract desires stung me with a primeval longing to touch, caress and kiss. But in her eyes was a void as dark as her leather jacket and as distant as the ground beneath us.

Now I am on the last leg of my lonely journey home. At last! But it is not over - not the journey, not the work, not even the yearning. The other day, when it was snowing in Chicago, I sat outside the downtown post office watching the snow from the warmth of my car. (Even the city is quiet when the snow is falling.) Inside of me was the din of techno music churning from the speakers. The poetry of the moment did not escape me.

TRAIL

I stumbled down the canyon wash as though I were a drunk on Vine Street. Every twisted root was a rattlesnake and every charred log a sleeping black bear. I could hardly imagine how water might find its way on this arid path.

We (*my thoughts and I*) went on that way for about an hour and a half. At last I came to the narrow pass where the Devil supposedly resides. I proceeded cautiously down the stone corridor imagining an ambush by U.S. Cavalry or some ragged frontiersmen forgotten in time. About halfway through I peered up from the grassy floor, my eyes tracking the towering rocks to the thin blue band of sky. At this moment I realized I was standing in the birth canal of the West Texas Mountains.

The realization was heavy, so I stopped there for a moment. I glanced down at my watch. I didn't know it then, but my faithful timepiece was nearing the end of its usefulness. Twelve noon, the time I promised myself I'd find a suitable spot to kick back, enjoy some water, and perhaps a snack. But the other side of this pass was beckoning me.

After thirty or so more yards I was on the far side of the canyon and alone in the shade. Right in front of me stood a small pole, on top of which a plaque was mounted. "End of Trail," it read. I chuckled and looked around. It seemed to me that I might decide for myself if this was the end. For as far as the eye could see the rocks continued in much the same fashion as they had for the last several miles. The only item missing was those neatly stacked rocks left at regular intervals by a ranger or Good Samaritan hiker to assure those without a keen sense of direction that they were not yet lost.

I found a nice comfortable rock to settle upon. It was in the shade, but I had no choice in the matter. It was the logical place, about ten feet from the sign indicating I had come to the end of the trail. So I sat quietly enjoying some water and peanut M&Ms.

I don't exactly recall my idle thoughts on that rock, but I do remember my mind being abuzz with romantic imaginings of days long gone when Texas was no more than a whisper in the western wind. I reminded myself, "You're here looking for Spring. You may have to look a little deeper, that's all."

"Would you mind keepin' it down over there?" the sign asked.

The sign spoke!

I took a deep breath, stood up, and peered over and around the rocks. A sweat stain was left where I was sitting.

"Keep what down?" I laughed out loud.

"The noise, the noise coming from your head. I haven't heard this much gibberish from one person since that Fred Savage kid hiked up here."

The sign just stood there.

"Don't just look at me. Say something!" he cried. (I say he because he sounded just like a guy from New Jersey named Marty.)

Believe it or not words come easy when you're talking to a sign. "What's your name?" I asked.

"Red Star. Red Star Cleveland," replied the sign. "Don't tell me yours. I bet you're William the Conqueror."

"You've got me pegged all wrong Red."

"Red Star!"

"I'm sorry, Red Star. Weren't you listening to what I was thinking?"

"Listening?! It sounded like a third grade music class. What the hell have you got going on in there?"

"Lots of stuff, but mostly romantic, poetic, listless imaginings."

"I thought I might've heard an angel singing," he snapped.

"Listen Red," I said.

"Red Star!"

"Pardon, I meant Red Star. I've never really talked to a sign before. What gives?"

"Yeah? Well I don't talk to many people either. Most can't even hear me. You just sorta looked lonely and that gray matter between your ears was making so much goddamned racket I just couldn't sleep."

"My apologies, Red Star. I came here to find peace of mind in the blossoming Spring. It's kinda strange how I run into you here at the end of the trail."

"Glad to oblige. You know there are worse places to be if you're a sign."

"Tell me about it," I said.

"I knew a couple of other signs before they put me up here, but they were mostly bathroom signs. Ya know, like 'Please Flush,' 'Put Trash In Its Place,' and my favorite: 'Sanitized For Your Safety.' Oh boy, she was a peach!"

An awkward silence followed this last exchange.

"So what exactly brings you here?" Red Star asked.

"Happiness."

"Happiness?"

"That's right, I'm looking for happiness."

"Have you found it?" the sign asked sincerely.

"In small bits and pieces. But I feel even if I'm not happy more often, I should at least enjoy my days a little more."

"You don't enjoy your life?" the sign coaxed.

"No. It is hard for me to say that, but it's true. I have things I look forward to – a day here or there; you know, traveling, or a visit with a friend. But day in and day out I feel depressed.

"I don't know," said the sign. "I've met a lot of people while posing for lots of pictures. Of 'em all you're one of a very few who seems to have a really good shot at happiness."

"How can you tell?"

"'Cause you know you're not happy and 'cause I think you have a good idea what will make you happy. Most people that end up here beside me don't realize whether they're happy or not. They're all distracted, lost in this world. Hell, most don't even say 'Hello' when I do talk to them!"

"Red Star, I've heard it said that knowledge comes but wisdom lingers. How did you get to be so wise?"

"I'm a sign," he chirped in that conceited New Jersey accent.

I slowly put my belongings back into my pack while reflecting on the words of Red Star. I didn't feel self-conscious in any way because I was certain Red Star had seen it all before. You know what I'm talking about – hiker reaches the end of the trail, looks around, enjoys a drink and heads back.

"Don't go if there's something else bothering you. I've got a long afternoon ahead and tomorrow's Monday. I may not see anyone until next weekend."

I laughed. "There's always the mule deer."

Red Star, quite seriously, replied, "There is one who's kinda cute. She doesn't come by often, but if she were to stop by right now I'd pretend you don't even exist."

I laughed again incredulously, and then pondered his words for a moment. Before even realizing it I blurted out, "What ever could exist between you and a deer?"

"My searching friend, happiness, like all things, is a perception. It exists within you."

So certain was his reply, I sat stupefied.

"Red Star, what do you mean a perception? I have books on my shelf I won't read because I don't understand them. Is this a matter of perception?"

"Absolutely. It is common belief we must react to our environment rather than meet it or exist within it."

"I don't follow."

"In football, if the defense shifts to the right and you're carrying the ball, then you cut left. You react. But in baseball if you're playing catcher and a runner is heading home, you'd better be there to meet him. In one situation you avoid, in the other you engage."

"And your meaning?"

"My meaning, lone hiker, is that the world exists within you. Me, the mule deer, and your happiness is a part of this. It is all as real as these rocks that surround us. But at the same time it is your perception or interpretation of the intelligence that surrounds us all."

"I'm overwhelmed."

"Am I a sign or intelligence expressed as wood and plastic?"

"Am I an intelligent expression of flesh and bone?"

"That I cannot answer."

"You're really screwing with my head Red."

"Red Star! And you've missed the point here. Your perception is taking over."

"Right."

"Take a drink and relax for a moment."

"My mind is exhausted."

"Yeah, well, how do you think I feel sittin' out here half-baked every day in the sun?"

"How long have you been here?"

"Long enough to have met all the mule deer in the park and too many scorpions."

I took a deep breath before continuing and on the exhale I spoke my piece. "So how do I escape my perceptions?"

"Look, I don't have all the answers," he said in a rather humble tone. "But your goal shouldn't be to escape your perceptions, only to alter them a little. Change comes slowly; just ask these mountains."

"I might," I muttered under my breath.

"It's impossible for you to escape this reality. Your mind won't tolerate it. But as things evolve, subsequent generations will not hold the same truths as we do, nor will they be hindered by our limits."

"I'm not so optimistic, Red Star."

"That doesn't really matter. But this shouldn't be depressing. There is no way for us to conceptualize the world as it really is. Therefore we try to encapsulate the moment. There is no right or wrong."

"You've taken me to the edge. I want to wrap my mind around it all, but then I see the abyss and my breath becomes shallow while my heart sinks."

"Don't separate yourself from it all. You, me, and the scorpions are all part of the infinite possibility."

"You're a damn talking sign, Red Star!"

"That is what your senses tell you. But maybe we are one and the same: intelligence, albeit expressed differently."

I sat there without speaking for what seemed like forever. The sun was now turning toward its downward arc. Red Star became less animated and I almost lost him, as you might lose the image in one of those magic eye prints sold at the mall.

Admittedly I liked what Red Star had to say. My own beliefs and perceptions had taken me only so far. I was far too myopic in my views. When I got to the precipice I had seen only entropy and infinite chaos. Now a sign that read "End of Trail" had calmed my mind like a fun diversion, but without the loss of consciousness.

"It is time for me to go, Red Star."

"Well I must say it has been a pleasure. Not too many folks make it this far up the canyon, and even fewer have anything meaningful to say. Hell, some even shove their tired asses right up in front of me."

"Thank you for the enlightenment. You have opened my eyes and now I must unlearn some things in order to move forward," I said smiling.

"Before you go would you mind pouring a little of your water on my face? It gets kind of dusty out here and I don't expect much moisture until next winter."

"You betcha, Red."

"Red Star!"

I met some other hikers on the way back through the canyon. While they all seemed quite friendly I didn't tell them about Red Star or the things he shared with me. I figured they might meet him without my help, or they may just have to find their way elsewhere. Anything's possible.

REINVENTING THE B:DRIVE

Saturday, only two weeks ago, I stepped off the plane and into her arms. I think she was expecting much more, but what she got was a trembling boy full of thought, a weir of emotions. In our embrace she could feel the thumping in my chest. (A better writer would have me come ashore, reminiscent of General MacArthur, with a flower in hand and the words: "This virtuous woman shall be taken, and I am the man to do it," reverberating from my lips.)

And so began my strange odyssey into life, love, and sex. It is astonishing what fear can do for people - not too much though - just more than is necessary. Fear is an easy emotion, much like loneliness. (With fear and loneliness it is always best to have a little patience.)

In the coming hours the awkwardness would wane but not her beauty. To know someone and to appreciate them from a distance is much different than having them in your pocket. To be fair to her I don't know women, and quite possibly I am a fool. My mind was so completely open that day I couldn't possibly escape its reaches. (How would you feel if you looked into someone's eyes and saw a room the size of a black hole sparsely decorated with a couple of ideas, thoughts, and colorless feelings?)

We kissed, but we talked more, and without real depth. It was like being in a city of the future where it is difficult to concentrate. In the preceding weeks she had worked tirelessly to pry me open, and when her wandering parakeet finally arrived, with equal effort she labored to stem the flood of my emotions.

Our phone calls were deep, relaxing, and occasionally funny; the emails, too. But where were those feelings in Chicago? I felt like the poet who had drowned while trying to kiss the moon in the water. What to do? What could we do? Our two worlds were on a windy city collision course. Accordingly we abandoned whiskey in favor of champagne and its misty promises. In doing so we were able to find a peculiar ecstasy on Sunday.

When it comes to women I am always a gentlemen, but boastfully admit there are exceptions. Unfortunately this weekend was not one of those occasions. I speculate when I say, much to her chagrin.

We took solace in our physical compatibility. In this arena I was little more than a pupil. Even in my confusion I must have done something right, for as the chasm opened between us so too developed an understanding that melted the bronze from my heart.

Bidding her farewell at that same airport where she rescued me was difficult only because we had figured out a connection. Our chance encounter months ago had now produced a rainbow. From her light came a physical connection which heretofore I had mistakenly regarded with the reverence of religion. And just maybe my raindrops surprised her a little because I don't think she was ever allowed to feel the tiny sensations in life.

I applaud anyone willing to follow a beckoning love. Yes, I know these are the words of a hyper-romantic, but that is part of me. If two worlds are able to become one, then you must never take the time to make up your mind about people.

BITTER AT MY LOVE.

I cannot believe what I am relating is my own story. This cannot be my life. But it is, and it pains me. I never thought I would grow tired of the warm body next to me. I remember when it was so new and so nearly overwhelming. To hold her was to live. And now...now she is poisoning my heart.

Truthfully she hasn't changed in the least. Her beauty is still evident in her face, her body, and her grace in these difficult times. The metamorphosis is within me.

Oh how I loathe this woman! Just breathing the same vapid air as her sickens me. I can barely stand the existence of our child, let alone fathom the idea of sleeping next to her.

I know there is no rationale for my feelings. Yes, I am afflicted with a horrendous disease. If the devil lives, it is in my cells.

I almost recall our blissful happiness, but it fades into dark at the very sight of our monstrous offspring. Our love was perfect, but my seed was sown in a demon valley. Together we produced a horrendous living thing that will not die but feeds on, nay devours, our once boundless love.

Now it is nearly gone. I blame her, my wife. How could she let such a creature grow inside her? Certainly I am not responsible for our hideous spawn.

Soon I will be no more, but not before the child takes all that I have. Dreams of the future have become nightmares of apocalyptic landscapes swept in human ashes. There was a time I counted myself fortunate, for not every man marries his true love. Yet such permanent ecstasy is not the privilege of a mortal man.

REFLECTIONS ON A TRAGEDY

I haven't been on the verge of tears so often since I was a child. My heart is torn, but it is a good thing. How can this be? What of those who lost their lives, their friends, and their family members? I know not what to say to assuage their anger, nor to relieve their pain. Yet today I live, where yesterday I existed. Feelings I thought lost but for the occasional romantic poem have surfaced like the adrenaline that surged within my veins as an adolescent. As the smoke cleared on the ruination of our society, the brilliance of life shone anew.

Some people like this country for what it has given them; others love it for the myth and power. But I love it for what it is: the grandest microcosm of all the world's diversity. Despite the internal divisiveness, at odd hours of crisis, the many become one.

HER

It is not as warm tonight and still the fire within, best described as longing, waxes and wanes with every beat of my heart. A beautiful woman on the street or at the gym is like a gust of wind that sends sparks throughout my body. Yet there is but one woman who is my constant, the burning ember that keeps my heart aglow. Her eyes betray her innocence, and bespeak an ageless sorcery. Though I am no more than a speck of dust in these transoceanic winds, I relish the burning, the dire yearning, as though it were hell's fury.

We've started across that line, and the most important thing is for me to remain myself.

I recall our first kiss for its softness, but visually I remember a slide show as I blinked for long intervals. Her nose, her teeth, her bottom lip, my lips, her top lip...slow, easy, soft, natural, memorable.

TRANSCRIPTION

I think I'm a bit closer to her and to understanding her. I felt a little self-pity this evening when she didn't call me back as soon as I expected. But when she did I became tender. At least that's how she made me feel. For some strange reason she came across the line even more feminine, more womanly, than I can ever remember. This alone caused a yearning within me, the likes of which I haven't felt for a long, long time. Don't let it frighten you, but it is so powerful that I want to consume her, or in other words, make her a part of me.

Forsaken among a patch of red berries.

I'm all stressed again and for no good reason. Unless not wanting to waste your life doing something you don't enjoy has some merit. I shouldn't complain because I do like some of it, and I'm sure I can make it fun. My goal is to be professional (the most) and laugh with my co-workers.

Being able to articulate how I feel is a great relief.

The last couple of days must have been extremely difficult for her. After our kiss I was a bit incredulous, perhaps to the point of being suspect. I truly wondered what had softened her heart to my advances. (Was it time? Experience? Fear?) Yet she must have been even more overwhelmed by it. The thought, "What have I done?" must have entered her mind. So for a couple of days she has had to face the prospect of our next meeting and that moment when I would want to kiss her again.

I am back in the fold.

I wish I could just go to sleep the way I did when I was a kid. But I want to see how it will all work out: the negotiations, the infrastructure, this season, and most of all this life.

Thus are the whims of the rich.

I'm just plain tired. My struggle is far less important than anything even a child could imagine – or is it? Every day I stave off savage attacks on my soul. I am victorious so long as there is something worth fighting for.

I think some people - maybe most - feel the presence of something intangible and powerful in their lives. They try to define and name this feeling. God, Allah, Yahweh, Buddha, and Jesus are but a few examples. A much smaller group of people simply revels in this feeling. Some ignore it or are incapable of feeling it.

Talk to me.

"You know I think you are a fool."

"Have you run out of kind words?" she replied.

"Almost. But my meaning is not harsh. I am sad because you are a fool. I don't know what to think of myself for adoring a fool."

(Long pause.)

"I suspected my words would elicit only silence. What goes on in your mind? You speak of the Phantom and how he urges Christine to join him in a new life. Am I the fool?"

What I should have done.

I should have reassured her. I should have pulled her close and told her not to worry, that I would be there. I should have kissed her tenderly and held her close. If I wanted her to be at ease I should have told her I know how she feels. Nobody should fear a burgeoning relationship.

All business…

I feel like if I work hard everything else will fall into place. I can't worry about how each individual behaves. For me, the most important things are sanity and my health. Sanity comes from having a life, and health from this sanity. I know if we communicate well, all will fall into place.

In the belly…

I know why we ignore the voice of reason. When I hear Led Zeppelin sing how she shook him all night long, I understand. And this is the same group that will leave her where the guitar is played.

POETRY

FIRST COLLECTION: 1992-1995

A POEM

"Who are you?" she pled.
"Does it matter?" he said.
"Can you see me?" asked she.
"In a manner of speaking," said he.
'Do you love me?" whispered she.
"Only when I touch you," mumbled he.
"Why do you treat me so?" she cried.
"I don't know," he lied.

ALONE

My shoulders are young, and they are broad.
But they cannot bear what all of us share.
Come, ease my loneliness...

BURY THE DEAD

Beautiful cemetery so green and alive,
your ancient mysteries I cannot contrive.
Enduring monuments rise up so high,
have you not forgotten you're supposed to die?

CAVEAT

When life tears my soul a gapin' hole,
I often put pen to paper.

And what I write, a horrendous sight,
seems to be romantic garbage.

Yet if you look beyond the love-sick song,
there is plenty of hidden meaning.

So if you read my work, don't go berserk,
and laugh or cry exceedingly.

CRYPTIC BURSTS II

Life: To know your own mortality and that you are part of something greater.

To be granted physical eternity would be a curse.

Myths allow us to open a mysterious realm.

In my wake I leave your body, preferring only your soul to keep.

He reached into the sky and handed her a star.
She dipped her hand into the sea and gave him life.

It all began innocently enough.

My body left long before. My soul remained forevermore.

The dead live in the blood of the living.

Few things scare me so, as those I do not know.

I am the beast who upon life does feast.

There is something about a girl who sings.

There is no written or spoken language in the world that can adequately express feelings.

We are going to find our future in our distant past.

I don't want to start a movement. I want to end one.

DEDICATION

I write to no one person but my lover;
where she is I cannot discover.

DESCARTES

The man about whom I write
was trapped in an age-old fight.
In life he found little meaning,
yet his fate kept intervening.
It sought to teach him love,
a concept he viewed from above.
Instead he turned to his learning,
but it only increased his yearning.

Over time the truth became clear.
However it only increased his fear.
For what he realized was this:

Life is only bliss,
And somewhere between animal and artificial is man...

"GREAT"

The days are long but I see her clearly.
I wonder if she knows I want her near me.
The sun rises, the sun sets;
she wakes thinking, and in sleep forgets.

On certain mornings it is her form I behold,
yet it is her soul that warms my cold.
The sun rises, the sun sets;
she wakes thinking, and in sleep forgets.

Scarred by eternity I pass her by,
concealing vulnerabilities I would deny.
The sun rises, the sun sets;
she wakes thinking, and in sleep forgets.

Behold her power to crush the darkness,
her hand extended in naked starkness.
The sun rises, the sun sets;
she wakes thinking, and in sleep forgets.

Our touch glows in the bleakest night.
love transcends all if not put to flight.
Joined as one in age-old repair;
we learn as much as we are willing to share.

The sun rises, the sun sets;
she dwells within me, in her I forget.

GOTHIC LOVE

The night both clear and cold,
did wax of stories often told.
The sanctuary stood still and dim,
as its bell tolled a perilous hymn.

A beautiful lady walked far from sight
avoiding paths of flooding light.
Within her darkness a tear did fly,
filled with a love unwilling to die.
For it is a terrible, terrible thing to adore
that which death can touch forevermore.

Now the beast swooped down on her as if the wind,
and ravaged her love with a savage grin.
He cut so deep he touched her heart,
but found true love he could not tear apart.

“Why do you hurt me so?” she cried,
“can you not see the pain I hold inside?”
“What I see is deep, dark despair,
that ages ago I, too, did share.
Come with me; you must surrender.
I know a place where love is tender.”

She looked into his wild eyes
and saw the truth only a fool denies.
Off they went to the land of the undead,
where as king and queen they made their bed.

INCRIMINATION

Sometimes I feel so volatile,
I could kill…kill with a smile.

IT SHOULD BE SO EASY

He resides on your surface;
I penetrate deep.
He desires you today,
I want you to keep.

JOIN US!

Today we opened a myth and grabbed the helm.
Suddenly we were in a mysterious realm.
Upon this strange sea, our conscience was set free,
and the mist hid nothing but you and me.

As we sailed we witnessed the miracle of birth,
and knew this realm was much like Earth.
We beheld the agony of violent death
as an Amazon warrior gasped her last breath.

Hercules appeared on the starboard side,
his strength rippling in the morning tide.
Across the bow the figure of Helen shone,
such beauty mortal man had never known.

Over the masthead flew a vision of love,
soaring ever so calmly was God's white dove.
But the Ancient Mariner saw it as did we,
and wounded it with an arrow from the sacred tree.

Undaunted we plunged into deeper waters
until the ship hit empty coffers.
Each glistening box displayed a crafted name,
a man or woman of eternal fame.

You begged me to read the names aloud,
so I started with the man of infamous shroud.
"Jesus," I read, but could not continue,
for we shuddered in the cold of this sinister venue.

"No more," I said, "I've seen mine,
"and I don't want to be part of this floating shrine.
"Let us plot a brand new course,
"one in which all people and all things are of an equal force."

"Spread immortality as if it were free,
"but add to it this one decree:
"the violators will suffer Ahab's fate,
"in this mythological world of love and hate."

"However, those who do willingly abide,
"we shall escort to the triple divide,
"where water flows along three paths,
"and there are no such things as epitaphs."

You pressed your lips against mine,
and the pact was sealed with approval divine.
The wind then blew in our direction
as we sailed on carrying infinite perfection.

MEMORANDUM #1

When you see me
remember, it's the little things.

When you hear me
remember, it's the little things.

When you court me
remember, it's the little things.

When you kiss me
remember, it's the little things.

When you smile at me
remember, it's the little things.

When you receive me
remember, it's the little things.

When you bury me
remember, it was the little things
(that made our relationship so special).

OBTHE1

"Where are you?" she said.
"Oh, but does it matter?" he said.
"In a manner of speaking," gasped she.
"Well then I'm peeping," laughed he.
"But you mustn't," whispered she.
"And why not?" implored he.
"Your eyes burn so deep," trembled she.
"That's because I love you," declared he.

SHE WHISPERS TO ME

She is the sea upon which I sail.
She is the way in a world without trails.
She is the moon that makes my skin rise.
She is the black cat with the hunter's eyes.

Everywhere I look she is all that I see,
except for a few others very similar to me.
It frightens me so to blink in her presence,
for I might fall in love with her silky-smooth essence.

Perhaps it scares me even more than it should.
So I stand here alone a tree of hard wood.
Then she sweeps through the forest a warm, gentle breeze.
Still her love blows me down and scatters my leaves.

"No," I call out as the tears come flyin',
"the world is much easier without lovin' and dyin'."
She smiles and whispers to me as only she can,
nods her beautiful head, and touches my hand.

"Be not afraid, I hold within me the light.
"Join your hand with mine and end this old fight."
She wipes away the lone tear from my eye,
creating the land, the lakes, and the sky.

Eternity groans as we unite under the sun,
for it knows the war we have already won.
No longer will the terror of loneliness strike me down,
because it ain't so easy, destiny, to uncrown.

THE FAIR LIFE

The shortest day of the year has come round.
It is dark and gloomy and devoid of sound.
I look out the window that faces the east,
checking ever-so-often for my personal beast.

My mind, so weary, moves neither here nor there,
and my morning eyes are transfixed in a stare.
"Lonely," I hear whispered on a far-off tide,
and I see fate grinning, as if me to chide.

What happened last night: good or bad?
In the dark of ignorance I am utterly sad.
Worry not, I say, drop all your cares,
you know very well life is not always fair.

TOO CLOSE YEARS (2 YEARS APART)

Ya know I've never been,
but I have to go, to Westminster Abbey.

I want to see the Gothic architecture rise,
that surely meant many a man's demise.

I want to hear the boom of the bells,
and the shrill sound of little girls' yells.

I want to climb the towers in the sky,
and with mixed emotions utter a sigh.

But I also want to see the history of our age,
and implore your help as we turn the page.

For in the evening mist will we be free
to carve a new existence for you and me.

I really, really need to go to Westminster Abbey.

WHAT PEOPLE WANT

What do people want the most?
The Father, the Son, and the Holy Ghost?

I decided to ask a friend.
"They want to know what comes in the end."

No, I thought, that cannot be.
They want the love of all and they want to be free.

"And you," asked my friend.
"Don't you wish to know about the end?"
"Of course not," I replied,
"That belongs to those who died.
"I want the love of people, and fame thereafter.
"For I possess knowledge of the hereafter."

"Think more clearly," came her voice from the heavens.
"You're ever so lucky I carry your sevens.
"Go now and share your life with her,
"and know that with me your fame is secure."

Thus fate smiled upon me.
Forever after I will hold the key.

1996

A.I.

I sit in wonder.
Often.
I wonder about you.
I wonder what will make me laugh tomorrow.
I wonder what makes me mad.
(In my angst I found Zeppelin. What will I do if the levee breaks?)
I wonder why Vegas is the modern Mecca.
So I have this affair with letters.
    (Yet nothing seems to improve with ink.)

Walpole tells me that the world is a tragedy to those who feel, but a comedy to others who think - I am on the fence.
I have been across the Continental Divide all the way to the City of Angels where I saw no divinities but the Ocean, who refused to swallow me.
Tolstoy tells the weeping Indian in Santa Fe, if he wants to be happy, be.
    (Now he sells his magic and soul on a chain.)
Therefore, I must refute Carlyle's theory that the essence of humor is love and not contempt.
    (At least as it now stands.)

Sometimes I get so tired of the hypocrisy, competition, and apparent neutrality that I want to scream.
    (Who would care? Who will read this?)
Snarl.
My savage innocence begets a poisonous clarity.

I sit in wonder.
When the sunshine lifts the foggy sadness, it will all have seemed so silly...

(ANGST) WHERE DO YOU WANT TO GO TODAY?

Angst-driven outta time,
sick of workin' for nickel and dime.
All fed up and no place to run,
his mind on the end his hand on the gun.

Thinkin' 'bout the deeper things,
temper flares and mood swings.
Life ain't 'bout the money and drugs,
sleepin' with women and cheerin' thugs.
And it ain't 'bout church and a home out beyond.
Don't give me that shit it's time to go on.

Somebody said, and I stooped to listen,
told me that life can be sweet for the kissin'.
The lesson it stuck and grew from within.
ignorance is bliss, mine is ruin.

Emotions are powerful...I feel them all.
Hope springs eternal until the fall.
Believe I won't, or can't, find the meaning.
Statue of Liberty soon will be leaning.

Life outta control nothing to stop it,
bullshit aside who will profit?
Those at the top fall from grace;
those that know shoot into space.

Joy feelin', pain cast aside,
gettin' on the train, headin' outside,
can't wait to see what's happenin' tomorrow,
there's still a chance I may end all the sorrow.

B. VOLIO

Methinks there is much reason to your rhyme,
yet to merely think hath no place in love.
I am no more in the throes of passion at this juncture in time
then are the clouds in the heavens above.
A man who art in love makes not sweet decisions,
his body oft marred by his delusional visions.

Still the table of life rolls out before me,
and is only part of the continent I must consume.
The question is not love, but be or not be.
Apocalyptic thoughts I must entomb.

FALL 1996

I have seen much, and heard much more still.
Yet many years will pass before I get my fill.
Each morn' rips me from peaceful slumber.
I trip into the world full of sadness and wonder.

Challenges abound for all that I see.
So few stop to simply be free.
They run here and there, not-so-mindless drones.
I understand the plight their vagueness bemoans.

Five years have passed since I let go the plan.
One day this year I awoke a grown man.
My fears and worries I resolved to let go.
No longer would I fear Fate's random deathblow.
So I resolved to see that place hinter,
where nary a snowflake visits in winter.

I know why there, but cannot admit
that it will look different with the same old shit.

LIBERTY

I believe nothing.
Nothing is so hopeless as this realization, revelation.
I believe nothing.
Where did the seed come from?
I believe in nothing.
This is not true; I believe in myself (at least I used to).
I believe in no one.
Only the people I've met seem real.
I believe not in not knowing.
I believe not in knowing.
Trapped I am until I believe.
Trapped I am until into my life I weave:
Someone…
Something…
Anything…
    To believe in…

I only doubt myself because this world exists within me.
I only contemplate this because I am free.

KEEPER OF THE "BE"

Peace comes in the night.
Only then are things put to right.
Yet the revealing day is sure to invade,
and as morning approaches the harmony fades.
For I am the Keeper of the "Be."
I am the symphony, and I am free.

Fate is heavy-handed on my soul.
Her faceless virtues I must extol.
I know the bitter hypocrisy that surrounds.
Still I rejoice in the wonder that confounds.
For I am the Keeper of the "Be."
I realize that simplicity is the key.

Destiny crowned me. I had no choice.
Now civilization pursues me to crush my voice.
So I speak bitterly, spitting wild thunder.
My mission is to build and not to plunder.
For I am the Keeper of the "Be."
I am heavy-hearted – I am uncertainty.

Try to find me on the plains,
and all you'll see is the lions' manes.
If you look especially close,
I am the bulging vein in the bulls' throat.
For I am Keeper of the "Be."
Both fear and rage abound inside of me.

LITTLE DITTY

Open hand, fly away,
gone forever, another day.

Heavy head and dry mouth,
Sandman says to head south.

And the truth slip slides away,
light breaks and shocks the day.

MIGHTY (WORDS TO A SONG)

Mighty I
Mighty She
Mighty He
Mighty We

Though mortal, Mighty I
Though frightened, Mighty She
Though lost, Mighty He
Though crazy, Mighty We

The mighty seraphs watch us, an awesome panoply.
Still the mighty feelings, unique, wound them invisibly.
For they cannot comprehend the dimensions in our lives –
a tear, a smile, a gasp, far mightier than knives.

You? They?
Mighty, too.
But ask me not how (don't be high brow)
They must figure it out
Jump, wiggle, and fuckin' shout
Jump, wiggle, and fuckin' shout

MOOD SWINGS

High moods, but slow steps,
longing for the time when I know what's next.
Filled with joy and then comes rage,
can't see the stars until I'm on stage.

Just when I think I've calmed myself down,
my blood boils and my feet move the ground.
My life is difficult 'cause I make it that way,
still I can't stand the fuckers that live for today.

Shock surges when I analyze my feelings.
If I acted on instinct I would bring down the buildings.
Yet with control I suppress my primal urges,
but what of those who can't, all Earth's human scourges?

I am no different…I tell myself so;
only that way can I make my little mind grow.
Solemn, stern, stolid, all bone,
if I don't learn to love, I'll die all alone.

MY LADY

My Lady writes to tell me about her day.
Such joyous news, and I feel so far away.
Her words reach through the screen and grab my heart.
"Where are you?" she writes.
She needs someone to scream at and to hug.
I smile, and then in a melancholic mood the cyberworld depart.
"If," the rotten word, inundates my mind.
Stop, think how, and the answer you will find.
I call, but she is out sharing her glee.
Oh god, if she only knew the colors she paints in my mind.
When I see her I will tell her. That scent! I can almost smell her.
But perhaps first I shall grab her, reach out and really nab her.
For words cannot convey, my thoughts they would betray.
Oh I must let her know that the feelings she cultivates in my heart be not my own...
Her beauty.

SIMPLY ROSE

She thanks me sincerely for the rose,
But am I the reason from the ground it grows?
Water goes to water, and life goes to life,
happiness springs from freedom, and laziness breeds strife.

Apathy is the seed of our country's new wealth.
like the honeysuckle in the spring,
it grows with incredible stealth.
And with no bloom it eventually becomes sterile, green indifference.

In the garden the seraphs guard god's roses.
Quadroons are pricked by the thorns of beauty.
In the dark three words come so easy.
Light will raze the dim ignorance.

No, thank you for the rose...I will simply be.

1997

NEVER IN THE MOMENT

I tried to steal you for inspiration, while standing at the station, in the valley of my home.
And though it was not bad – in fact the best I've ever had – I now know the terror of my error.
If you could only see how I shudder when my thoughts recoil in search of my muse - god I'm confused.
I wonder if I'm a traitor, so I ask the addict if I've hit my nadir – *No Answer.*
Now as I lay alone to sleep, but not yet that deep, I search for consolation.
Should I see her again, maybe now but maybe then, I would ask to share her inspiration, while standing at the station, in the valley of my home.

BRILLIANCE

How fragile is the true me?
The tide licks the sands, people on the strand, raging is the band.
All round me is wealth; keen are those who have it.
Practice stealth and you may have it, but beware those who grab it.
No, never mind me, how fragile is the true me?
Work sucks me in, keepin' busy in the raging din.
No need for money, except maybe to find a honey.
That lust kills the feeling, awake staring at the ceiling, say your prayers kneeling.
Wealth would kill me. How fragile is the true me?
Notice the difference in the people: skin, hair, eyes, steeple.
It takes so little to sway me, don't forget the late fee, ass-out and crazy.
Wanderlust a nemesis, how fragile is the true me?
Precarious as falling in love, tighter than a leather glove, simple, white, floating drug
Change for its own sake or not at all, variations in the design are the artist's call.
To find happiness in chaos is no small task, eternity in the present and the person behind the mask.
I'm told that there is a right way, each day.
The gods favor those who die young.
How fragile is the true me?

HER NAME WAS SALLY RIDE.

Her name was Sally Ride.
Deep thoughts she did confide.
In a song, a verse, a word;
so powerful her voice, though seldom heard.

Then came the day when she rolled the dice,
went to LA where it's always nice.
Met some people and played her tunes;
they offered her the sun, the stars, the moon.

She agreed to put her soul out on a disc,
a successful venture, though an awesome risk.
As certain as a wanted kiss,
her brilliant talent could never miss.

Though I have not seen her since the move,
her deep lyrics still cut my groove.
And I wonder if I ever had the chance,
would she even grant me just one dance?

Now I hear people say that Sally sold the farm,
met the devil and borrowed his charm.
But most people aren't quite so pensive,
Sally and I are both real sensitive.

INSTANT REFUND TOAST

To Instant Refund's past success,
and to a future even brighter.
To Carroll, Stan, Charles, Chris,
and to Floyd who's quite a fighter.
To cold and snowy days,
and nights that are even longer.
And of course to all the problems,
and to Tom Glaze, who makes us stronger.
To Daddy (Fez) & Mommy (Robin),
and to all the Instant Refund staff.
May IRTS make a million,
and kick some H & R Block Ass!

RED LAND

In the morning just before day breaks,
fading shadows enter softly and dance till he's awake
His mind's so clear he admires their serenity,
but what of his lost muse off to join the enemy?

Life is seamless; life is sore
Images of last night seep into every pore.

Her silent path wilts in the blazing sun
Gone forever the sweet taste of her tongue.
She has no beginning and does not end
Where can she go? Where has she been?

Life is seamless; life is sore
Images of last night seep into every pore.
Pen in mouth and fire in mind,
he dreams of a land absent in time.

His anger grows but his courage wanes,
wounded at heart, on him life gains.
She has no beginning and does not end.
His love won't bring her back home again.

Life is seamless; life is sore
Images of last night seep into every pore.
Pen in mouth and fire in mind,
he dreams of a land absent in time.

SILVER SLIVER

I'm in a:
Screaming, silver sliver.
In my mouth a taste so bitter;
Through my bones I feel a shiver.
Heavy thoughts must be considered.

All around me are:
Sleepy, silent sailors
in a creepy, crowded cabin
trapped thick among the willows,
and the puffy, floating pillows.

I can see:
Sweet, serendipitous sleep.
If you can fly no need for feet.
Lost for them like a golden chance,
eternity only a weapon of religious trance

Can't you hear the:
Sardonic, simple song
with no possibility of right or wrong?
Why can't I enjoy their bliss?
Beneath me the engines hiss…

SOUTH DAKOTA SONG (THE LINGERING PANGS)

My lust for her is as strong as ever.
My love not so great, my ties I sever.
Physical boundaries I long to explore.
Could there be harm if she approves the deal?
Moot thoughts besiege me. How I long to feel.
Consciousness rides me…I am so sore.

1998

A DEPARTURE

The tanned leather hide
hangs from my wrist,
a woven gift unwillingly, unwittingly
given by a bovine creature.
All the same, the suffering foregone,
the thin, sinewy straps have taken
new life among the hairs of my arms.
Beads woven into the design
add spice to this new life,
and the bamboo shoots, over
time, warped by water, and fall off.
What does it symbolize?
Anything?
Would I trade it for a Rolex?
Probably not – that would be something to worry about
I don't worry about this.
Like me it simply is.
So I'll proudly wear it,
let the world change and tear it.

AT DAWN

On a street corner in any old town
the clickity-clack and the city sounds,
Stands my fate and she's all alone.
The blood in my veins just turns to stone
As the rusted wheels in my mind whirl and buzz.
They tell me about love and all that it does.
I try not to hear all of their crap
for my salvation lies in that lovely sap

Though the cold rain begins to pour,
I leave the dryness of my sheltered door.
Soon her name will leap from my lips.
As the music plays my hands fall to her hips.
Then in the morning the dawn of our love,
she and I will be like hand and glove.

CRAZINESS

Moping, Melancholy, Madness
Strong, Silent, Sadness
Hungry, Hollow, Happiness
Yearning, Yawning, Youthfulness
Talking, Trying, Treasonous
Wanton
Wild
Wonderin'
Whisperin'
I see the notes.
They don't spell "music."
I can only hear it if you sing it.
"Are you a seraph?" asks the angel.

DEPRESSION (1)

Being smart is of little consolation,
and so increases my isolation.
Then with the rain comes gray depression,
a smiling face, but furtive aggression.

DICKENS

I must thank Pip for that simple thought.
I do not think it ever occurred to me.
In a world so crazy and shallow with rot,
letting someone love you sets you free.

GRANDPA

There's a peaceful love in letting go
my soul a brand new day.
A mortal man I love so much
has up and flown away.

I CAN PITCH FOUR OR FIVE HUNDRED MILES AN HOUR.

I can pitch four or five hundred miles an hour.
Don't be sour.
I imagine you could do the same.
What do you mean insane?
It really is quite simple.
Let go the limits.
See the world through a lizard's eyes.
Surprise!
Go without those shackles.
Lay them aside.
That thought only serves to make you human.
Over the horizon the sun is loomin'.
That old crap is a tool for the unwise,
so powerful it keeps the masses in line.
But don't be fooled,
for it is they their chains entangle.
Forgiveness of base imperfection leads to personal insurrection – Wink!
Just walk away.
Ahead the new day.
A swing…
and a miss!

JOURNEY

A luckier man I know not one,
afloat in a marsh, on his hip a gun.
Daddy haunts me, the eerie echo in his head.
With heavy heart his journey he doth dread.

He longs for the sky a California Blue,
and in his lover's eyes the very same hue.
The sun will burn the swamp mist from his mind.
Gone are the shackles that so long did bind.

KEROUAC (1)

I read on because I am not sure if it is complete and utter brilliance, or the ramblings of an intoxicated, depressed, and spoiled neo-intellectual.
Perforce.
I want to believe it is the former.
We are not so different.
A haunting suspicion makes me suspect the latter.
How arrogant can someone be to think their stories of young over-sexed, irresponsible, junkie Americans hold the keys to salvation of humankind?
Let alone make a living at this?
That I understand...Capitalism makes little sense.
Still the plight and onus of the artist does not escape me.
It is I.
Allowances, no, open-mindedness, brings acceptance and soon appreciation.
How come there is no mention of our attempts to purchase and hoard natural beauty?
Natural, Physical, Temporal
I turn the page.

KEROUAC (2)

No Kerouac tonight, or dinner for that matter.
A little ice cream from the DQ and some iced tea will have to do.
In my head are so many possibilities,
I'm frightened by it all.
Like holding water…don't squeeze…
A sacrifice here…there…
When…Where?
The top is my goal.
I'm filled with such soul.
Here my feet on the ground,
treasonous thoughts do confound.
Grasping, rasping…don't want to let go (spill!) all the opportunities.
But I must rest.
Way past midnight,
skip Kerouac's insight.

LIMITLESS

Happiness is the dreams that fall into space.
Three hundred years past is endless naturescape.
Grueling is life when opportunity is missed,
Guernica your soul when your lover is pissed.
Chaos is the future of our uncertain path,
idyllic the gods and their self-serving wrath.
Hope is a medallion laid into my soul.
Greed is the bacteria that creates a hole.
Nowhere is the course upon which I write.
Limitless is the goal, therein my delight.

LONELY (1)

Lonely, alone, wealthy and unfulfilled,
life in that shell has got to be hell.
My hand against the wall and the other holding my brain,
out through my eyes I let my soul drain.
I've got no direction...I ain't got nothing to lose.
Might even trade my paycheck for some extra time to snooze.
'Cause whether I'm working or sleeping, the dreams are the same.
Can't wait for the day when I've mastered the game.

LONELY (2)

All is good in our techno-prosperity.
I don't want to be alone when I am despairing.
With greater men I shall even the score,
take mine standing, a gentleman the more.

LONELY (3)

It's over...
no longer a slave to my misgivings.
From what hell these doubts arose they are returned.
Almost a crazy man, a lover spurned.
What's to worry? I have but one life to give.
The river is rising – I choose to live.
Silver Socket Sets
Shiny Saddle Shoes
Soft, Sultry Skin

MELANCHOLY

The digital song dances in my head.
Material wealth it offers to spread.
Down this path do I want to be led?
Analytical chains are what I dread.

META (1)

Oh how I long,
when I hear that song,
to become one with it!
That's just a thought in my crazy mind,
here on Earth serving a lifetime.
Wanna hear another?
Sometimes I wish I were the only human on the planet,
and for a moment in space that's the case.
Pop!
Again one of six billion...but individual.
There are so many stars.
Bizarre.
I can name a lot of them...no matter.
Peace I find in my soul.
That is my goal.

META (2)

I have a vision:
A world of precision.
There is no decision;
no need for revision.
My soul in collision.
I've made no provision.
Enough.

METABOLIC CRAZINESS

No, not a maze, a smoggy haze.
Roads looped, paths layered, gates open.
Which way to go?
I am so slow.
Your breath is heavy – a lack of oxygen?
Don't ask such questions, rather offer suggestions.
I don't mind the work, but I hate to suffer
metabolic craziness.

MONEY (1)

The coin falls to the table.
Click…click…click…heads.
It reads "In God We Trust."
So goes our legacy.
There is no legitimacy
without money.
Don't our laws seem a little funny?
Everywhere I go,
everything I see,
becomes a dollar sign to me.
Let's write a little song
and take it to the bank.

Many of my friends speak Money,
but I am not affluent;
although I could make that my goal.
When I was younger
everything I did had the purest motivation.
Ovation!
Now nothing I do with my day
is taken seriously without thought of pay.
I walk the tight rope of sanity.
The Gold Standard holds only calamity.
Can I have both
material wealth and infinite scope?

MORNING

A pop and a click,
then the spinning of a disc.
Out come the words,
the sounds of the birds.
Are you given to fly, or have you got a wish?
I rise with the melody and then I fill my dish.
Tea, lemon, sugar and out the door.
I leave the man for the business whore,
making my move in the morning rush.
Turn up the radio and I can't hear 'em cuss.

PHILOSOPHER

What do you think a philosopher is?
Images of old fellows flood the mind.
The Greeks surely follow.
The depressed…God is dead.
I am and I write.
Words give my thoughts flight.
I see the dove and I dream of love.
I cross the river and know its lesson.
It is for me that our earth beckons.

PRIMAL LOVE FEELING

My yearning is so intense,
my awe immense.
When I see you my pulse races,
the lust it chases,
A primal feeling now grows unchecked.

SILLY SALLY

Silly Sally Sipper
with the red and yellow zipper.
Oh how I want to trip her!
With my boot I sure could flip her,
but I think I'd rather kiss her.

SNAKE BITE EYES

Snake bite eyes in a blue wave trap
breeze in my hair as the sun burns black.
Many different styles strewn for miles,
balls in the air, chartreuse flare.
Toes sifting the stuff of transistors' glass,
feeling lost in the world. Will this too pass?

SONG OF PLASTIC

Song of plastic, stream of thought.
The movie reminds me of our predatory nature.
Can we conceive of a life that is not violence,
a being benign to all other life?
The train out my window is squealing to a stop,
Olean, cars, coal – currency of the regional economy.
And so ends El Dia del Padre.
I have closed the book on Mardou.
Conscious thoughts recorded, I dream of polyethylene.

SPUTTERING GENIUS

Brilliance breaks across my bow,
a crashing and cracking wave in glass.
Wide I steer of smaller minds,
a captain at twenty-five…
My course altered,
my path adjusted,
only in the physical…
By the idyllic…
Consumed by the tragedy of their lives…
Too eager to embrace their death...

TAX SEASON

Chaotic brother
I know none other.
When the whistle blows,
when the bell sounds,
when the call comes.

Where's the glory?
Heard the money story?
I want the recognition.
Can't spell it with numbers.
Ah, my talent slumbers.

Wake! Wake like spring born from winter!
My mind will splinter!
The contract honored,
I will explode upon my path,
leaving pebbles for the revenue agents.

TRAINS

Click. Clack.
The train on the track
The groaning cars.
The morning stars
Smell that diesel
The horn cuts the air
Rust falls like rain
And the wheels come to life
Now the semaphore is green
The gate falls in line
All's runnin' along just fine
The train on the track
Click. Clack.

WHO'S TO BLAME?

Who's to blame? What a shame!
Such excess makes me nauseous.
You look out. Try looking in.

1999

!

If she wants me to stop she must ask,
but I don't think she will.
Love…perhaps.
Passion the culprit,
insatiable my desire. I breath fire.

@HOUSTON

Who are you?
Who am I?
I look up.
You compliment my eyes. ("You have the most beautiful eyes!")
Very nice.
Your kindness burns straight through to my core.
Without even another word, I could promise my eternal love to you.
(It wasn't just the words; it was your face. You smiled when I looked up at you.)

A.S.

Do you really want to be remembered,
dragged through the ages and dismembered?
Arrogant men scar the Earth for immortality.
Still she forgives this pretentious formality.

Now suppose that I die without even one dime,
rebuked by eternity, scorned by all time?
Such a freedom is rare, even to the last.
So sweet is the dream, I am left near aghast.

But I bet if you'd let me, I could give you a kiss,
make you forget all this nonsense in sincere eternal bliss.

CHARMA

Why can't I find a Dharma,
the type who will disarm ya?
Perhaps it is my Karma,
or my stranger brand of charma!

FRAUDULENT DEITY

She makes me feel like a deity,
albeit fraudulent.
She seeds my mind with metaphysical germs.
They grow wild on fertile ground.
She reaps, nay steals, the harvest from my heart,
and I am empty.
Seduced,
I love her stinging wonder.
She fears my illimitable spirit
and refuses, refuses, to acknowledge my human desires and frailties.
I guess she will not make love to gods...

I AM

I am
too tired to share the brilliance.
I am not
afraid to fall in love.
I know
this guy in California who is.
I know
this girl in Ohio who is.
(I must
complete a thought!)
I doubt
they have much else in common.
I told them
love is one million emotions,
guided by Fate, policed by Devotion,
I hear
fear, uncertainty, and despair.
I am angry!
Check their list of excuses:
she sings without reason;
good will he abuses
!

MY DAY

I've got lots of spiders in my room.
Before I even think about it my thoughts go zoom,
and I am running in the woods.
Through my head fly "shoulds" and "coulds,"
and coasting in to my surprise,
a four year old holding my first prize.
I take the daisy and thank her kindly.
Then proudly I walk to my car, but also blindly.
I strain to pay attention to all the folks,
while in my mind I laugh at my buddy's jokes.
Next I'm in the car and out on the road.
In front of me a beautiful woman I behold,
For now the highlights of my day are told.
I see her in the mirror to her left and to her right,
three images to compose her fairness.

SCARED STIFF

This fear of dying can never last.
Like you on Earth it will surely pass.
And all that's left is dust and bone.
Perhaps a name, too, carved on a stone.

SONNET BLUE

Bright and blue, so chilly too,
came to your door and evermore,
Stunned was I by your beauty through,
Emphatic praise I delight to pour.

A key to turn, then rubber burn.
Out on the sea, just you and me.
A laugh, a smile, the story turns,
then quietly I sip my tea.

An hour early, but nowhere to go.
Not sure of God but inspired by Fate,
we delight a common thread to sew.
How much longer can I wait?

The songs are magic and the timing right,
I think we could dance all damn night.

WATER TOWER LOVE

Are you always so pretty?
A smile...A blush...Oh my! – A tear.
Here come seven smiles in seven styles.
There are no superlatives in life
except you.
Ours is a love affair.

2000

BEEP

Beep…
Beep…
Beep-Beep…
Beep-Beep-Beep-Beep…
Do you think you're better off alone?
How do you ignore this urge?
Someone please talk to me…
No hay palabras. (There are no words.)
Beep…
Beep…
Beep-Beep…
Beep-Beep-Beep-Beep…
Oooooooh…

DOCUMENT3

The wind blows fiercely tonight
and I can't get close enough to you.
Who would have thought that happiness lives in the desert?
Who wouldn't mistake this place in my heart for Babylon?

I turn my thoughts over and over.
With dry lips they say, "Come and get it."
Touching you is electric goose bumps in sweet honey;
your smile, white-golden pearls in crimson candy.

I dive into your waters without a care.
Tears, clear and salty, are washed away.
I can feel the mountains below us.
The flowers on your tongue invite the bees.

Calm meadow grass lies still in the silver moonlight;
you whisper, "Let go your heart."
The frantic city surges in our consciousness,
the feeling punctuated by the lonely cry of the coyote.

Like hushed cymbals we are calmed.
Lying on a soft bed of ferns among the ancient timber
your butterfly eyes powder my nose with musty aromas.
Do you always purr at the end of a dream?

REJECTED TITLES

Freddie Killed the Cat
As Long as it's Free
A Little Something Different
Semi-Automatic
Rogers & B:Drive
Soup for the Sideburns
Ophelium, Ophelia
B:Drive, B:Drives – masc. 2nd Decl.
Meatloaf Tuesdays
Write by Night
A Tribute to Aaron Feuerstein of Malden Mills
It's Not My Gift to Dance
Shave Me
B:Drive and the Seven Dwarfs
Green Tobacco
In B-Minor
And So It Goes
Beyond the Crystallized Collective
As You Might (See Things)
Killer
Sacrilegious Red Grapes
Rewind
Gotcha! (Got You)
Full Ahead (Forward)
Singing Into a Bell
How I Work
Epiphenomenon
Brain Chemistry
Conceptual Imprisonment
Mechanisms

Quite Simply
Nickel
Based on a Linear Model
Looking For the Blue Oxen
All Perception
Thick
How It Works
On My Back
Method
All Together
Prelude
Pomegranate
Savage Innocence
What Would Witter Do?
Writing Uphill
Poor Man's Radio
On The Verge of Ice
A Technician with Feeling

ACKNOWLEDGEMENTS

There is so little we can ever accomplish alone. This collection may be a summation of individual writings, but the inspiration, organization, and editing came from many sources.

Annette S.
Italo Calvino
Dad
F. Scott Fitzgerald
Joseph Heller
Ernest Hemingway
Jane H.
Joe K.
Jenny M.
Kelly F.
Jack Kerouac
Marti M.
Henry Miller
Mom
Peter M.
Tom Robbins
John Steinbeck
Kurt Vonnegut

Thank you.

www.ingramcontent.com/pod-product-compliance
Lightning Source LLC
LaVergne TN
LVHW011912080426
835508LV00007BA/494

* 9 7 8 0 9 9 6 8 1 2 0 3 0 *